Herbs and Medicinal Plants
by Roger Phillips

assisted by Jacqui Hurst
and Martyn Rix

GW00675828

Elm Tree Books London

INTRODUCTION

Aim

In this book we have aimed to photograph and describe a comprehensive list of the important herbs and spices that can be grown and used in the British Isles and Europe.

How to use this book

The plants illustrated are in two main sections: first, culinary herbs (up to page 111), then important medicinal herbs, many of which are poisonous. In the first section plants are arranged roughly according to their culinary importance, beginning with the most popular flavouring herbs and spices. In most cases one photograph illustrates the herb growing in its natural habitat or in a garden, indicating its size and shape; the other shows the plant laid out so the details can be seen easily and clearly. Sometimes hybrids, cultivated forms or closely related species are featured. The actual date of the photograph is given on the caption.

What is a herb?

A herb is an aromatic plant of which the flowers, leaves, stems, seeds and sometimes the roots are used for culinary or medicinal purposes. For culinary purposes it is preferable to use herbs while they are fresh because they have a much stronger flavour, whereas spices are more pungent when dried. For medicinal purposes herbs can be used fresh, dried or processed.

The photographs

The studio photographs were taken on a Bronica 120 format with a 75 mm lens. Scale: O is 1 cm. The field photographs were taken on a Nikon

Arctic Thyme growing in Finland

FM camera with a 50 mm lens, occasionally with close-up attachments. The film was Kodak Ektachrome 64 ASA in both cases, but when used outdoors it was pushed one stop in development.

Glossary

calcareous	containing chalk or limestone
court-bouillon	water and herbs boiled together
decoction	solution of a herb
diaphoretic	promoting sweating
mucilage	a slime formed on the surface when wetted
rhizome	an underground, usually creeping, stem
rust (disease)	a fungus disease of leaves, usually showing as reddish-brown pustules
tisane	herbal tea
umbel	many stems arising from same point, forming flat-topped head of flowers
vermifuge	a herb which purges intestinal worms

Wild Thyme photographed 11 July

Wild Thymes

The Greeks named this herb 'thymon', meaning fumigate, and they used it for incense in their temples. There are over 100 forms developed from Wild Thyme, also known as **Mother Thyme**. The leaves contain an oil, thymol, which is a disinfectant and aids digestion of fatty foods. The Romans bathed in thyme water to give them courage and vigour whereas the Highlanders and Islanders believed the smell alone was sufficient to bolster their courage. All the wild plants have a milder flavour than the garden varieties.

Wild Thyme, *Thymus serpyllum*, is a small native shrub only found in the Brecklands or East Anglia. It grows to 5 cm, and flowers from July to August. Common Wild Thyme, *T. drucei*, is a native mat-like shrub and is found on dry grassland, dunes and rocky places throughout Britain. It grows to 7 cm and flowers from May to August. **Large Wild Thyme**, *T. pulegioides*, thrives on calcareous soil in the south-east of England. It grows to 25 cm, and flowers from July to August.

Top left, *Thymus herba-barona*, top right, *T. albus*, bottom left, *T. drucei*, bottom right, *T. polytrichus*, photographed 11 July

Common Thyme photographed 11 July

Garden Thymes

The pungent tang and aroma of garden thyme is excellent added to poultry and game stuffings, sausages and meat stews and casseroles cooked slowly in wine sauce. It is an essential ingredient of bouquet garni, providing a background flavour for soups and vegetable dishes. Take cuttings in April or May and plant in light, well-drained soil, or sow the seeds during the spring.

Common Thyme, *Thymus vulgaris*, is a bushy evergreen perennial with small dull green leaves and mauve flowers which bloom in June. 'Silver Posie', a popular hybrid, has pink flowers and silver variegated foliage. **Golden Thyme**, *T. vulgaris* 'Aureus', has whorls of pink flowers and golden leaves and forms a fragrant ground cover. *T. vulgaris* 'Frangrantissimus' is an upright plant with pink blooms and grey leaves, and smells of balsam. *T. azoricus* has spiky bright green leaves and forms a dense carpet.

Upper left, *Thymus hirsutus*, middle, *T. vulgaris*, lower, *T. rotundifolia*
photographed 11 July

Lemon Thyme, Silver Posie, photographed 30 June

Lemon Thymes

Lemon thymes have broader leaves than other garden varieties and bees find their spicy scent very attractive. The flavour is mild but has a lemony piquancy which is splendid for stuffing fish and seasoning vegetables, particularly potatoes, and adds an unusual tang to fresh fruit salads and summer drinks. Picked when in flower, this herb dries well and retains its flavour.

Lemon Thyme, *Thymus × citriodorus*, is an upright evergreen perennial with pink flowers which blossom in June. It grows to 25 cm and has a strong aroma. *T. × citriodorus* 'Aureus', a bushy perennial with a mild odour, has pink flowers and variegated golden leaves; *T. × citriodorus* 'Variegatus', has silver variegated foliage, but these two species are liable to revert. Popular creeping hybrids are: 'Creeping Lemon', with large lemon-scented leaves and pink blooms; 'Doone Valley' with purple flowers and golden variegated leaves and 'Lemon Curd' with grey-green foliage and a strong perfume.

Top left, *Thymus citriodorus*, top right, Silver Posie, bottom left, Golden King, and bottom right, Boothmans Var. photographed 30 June

Field Mint photographed 16 June

Wild Mints

Perennial herbs with whorls of small purple, lilac, pink or white flowers. The species are variable and they hybridize freely which makes them difficult to identify. The flavour varies according to the soil and climate in which they are grown. There are three common mints found growing wild but their taste is considered inferior to the popular cultivated varieties.

Water Mint, *Mentha aquatica*, thrives in swamps, marshes, along river banks and damp woods in Britain, except in the Highlands. It grows to 80 cm and flowers from July until October. It has a pungent minty aroma when crushed. **Horse Mint**, *M. longifolia*, is rare and rather local in the British Isles. It is scattered along damp roadsides and waste places. It grows to 75 cm and flowers from June to September. **Corn** or **Field Mint**, *M. arvenis*, was commonly found in arable fields and hedgerows but is becoming scarce. It grows to 50 cm and flowers from May to October.

Water Mint photographed 16 June

Horse Mint photographed 10 July

Apple Mint photographed 10 July

Round Leaved Mints

Mints have creeping rhizomes which spread rapidly unless confined or grown in a container. They are easy to propagate by dividing the runners in spring or autumn and planting them in a moist, light but rich soil in partial shade. Replant mints every two to three years.

Apple Mint, *Mentha rotundifolia*, is similar to **Bowles Mint**. It can be found in ditches, roadsides and waste places in the southwest of England. It grows to 60 cm and flowers from July to September. It has large, round, hairy leaves, and is hardy and less prone to rust disease than other mints. Some consider the combination of apple and spearmint the finest flavour for cooking. The woolly texture disappears with chopping. Add to summer drinks, fruit salads or make chocolate and mint ice cream. **Pineapple Mint**, *M. rotundifolia variegata*, has cream variegated leaves and forms attractive groundcover.

Top left, Pineapple Mint, *Mentha rotundifolia* var. with Apple Mint, *M. rotundifolia* photographed 10 July

Peppermint photographed 29 May

Long Leaved Mints

Popular culinary plants in Britain are rarely used on the Continent because the sharp minty flavour does not blend with other herbs.

Spearmint, *Mentha spicata*, a commonly cultivated pot herb, can be found as a garden escape in England. It grows to 60 cm and flowers from July to September. Make into mint sauce or jelly and serve as a condiment with lamb. Cook a sprig with new potatoes, peas and carrots or scatter finely chopped leaves over salads, courgettes or cucumbers to add a refreshing bite. **Curly Mint**, *M. crispa*, is a decorative form of Spearmint. **Peppermint**, *M. × piperita*, is a hybrid between Watermint and Spearmint. The high oil content, menthol, is a renowned flavouring for desserts, sweets such as peppermint fondants, cordials and liqueurs. Peppermint tea is drunk as a tonic and helps digestion. **Eau de Cologne Mint**, *M. citrata*, has a distinctive fragrance and is added to summer drinks and pot pourris.

From left to right, *Mentha citrata*, *M. crispa*, *M. spicata* photographed 10 July

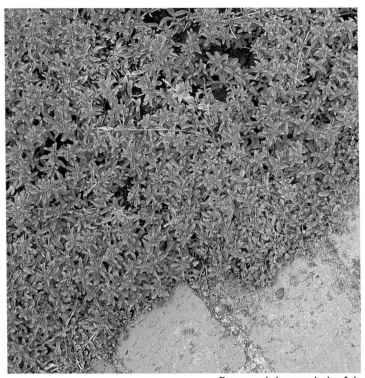

Pennyroyal photographed 17 July

Pennyroyal
Mentha pulegium differs from other species of mint because it is a small, procumbent plant which only grows to 20 cm. It flowers from August to October. Its botanical name is derived from the Latin, *pulex*, meaning flea. It was a custom to wrap the fresh herb in a cloth which was placed in a bed to drive away fleas and bugs. The mint was then renewed every week. Nowadays, Pennyroyal is not used in the kitchen because of its pronounced, slightly acrid taste and aroma, but it is the basic flavouring herb added to North Country black puddings, hence its local name – Pudding Grass. Pennyroyal tea was an old remedy for colds and whooping cough.

Corsican Mint, *M. requienii*, is a prostrate creeping mint from Corsica and Sardinia. It has a strong peppermint perfume.

Lower lefthand corner, *Mentha requienni*, with *M. pulegium* photographed 17 July

Purple Sage photographed 10 June

Sage

Salvia officinalis is a hardy perennial shrub, native to the North Mediterranean coast. It grows to 50 cm and flowers from June to July. Take cuttings from a mature plant in late spring and place in a sunny position in well-drained soil, or propagate by layers: peg down the branches and cover with earth, then when rootlets are established cut them away from the old plant.

The name *Salvia* is derived from the Latin *salvare*, meaning to save. It was a popular medicinal herb used mainly as a remedy for coughs, colds and fevers and as a general tonic. It was customary to add sage to cheese to improve the flavour and this is continued in the north where they make Sage Derby Cheese. It is used to flavour meat dishes and sage and onion stuffing for duck, goose or pork. Chopped fresh leaves can be added to green salads, or a small sprig put into fruit drinks, wine, cider cups or Pimm's.

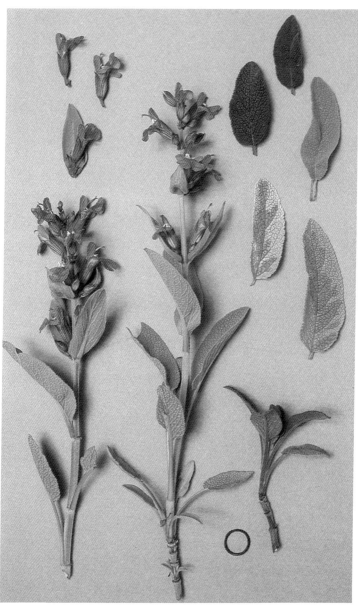

Salvia officinalis with leaves from the purple and variegated hybrids photographed
10 June

Clary photographed 14 August

Clary

Salvia sclarea is a biennial herb from southern Europe. It grows to 1 metre and flowers from May to September. Sow seeds in spring in light, well-drained soil. The leaves will be at their best for use during the following winter and spring.

The English name Clary is derived from the Latin *clarus*, meaning clear. It has a strong, aromatic scent and because it tastes rather bitter it has fallen into disuse. In Germany the leaves were combined with elder-flowers and added to wine to give a Muscatel flavour, whereas in this country they were used as a substitute for hops. The fresh leaves can be fried in a sweet batter and eaten with sugar and lemon juice. Nowadays, Clary is mainly grown commercially in France to extract its oils, which are used as a fixative in perfumes.

Salvia sclarea photographed 14 August

Wild Marjorum photographed 30 July

Oregano

Origanum vulgare is a native perennial, prolific on calcareous soil in England and Wales, and found on slopes, in meadows, hedgerows and scrub. It grows to 65 cm and flowers from July to September. It is easily grown from seeds sown in April or by root division taken in spring or autumn.

Oregano is also known as **Wild Marjoram**. There are a number of varieties of this plant, and this may have caused the confusion about its correct name. In southern Italy this herb has a pungent, spicy aroma and taste, whereas in cooler climates it lacks this peppery tang. The leaves should be gathered just before the flowers open. They can be added fresh to vegetable dishes (aubergines, courgettes, salsify and carrots) scattered over salads, mixed with basil and served with tomatoes or used to season seafood recipes.

Wild Marjorum, *Origanum vulgare* photographed 30 July

Bush Basil photographed 17 July

Bush Basil

Ocimum minimum is a low bushy annual from India. It grows to 16 cm and flowers in July and August. The leaves are ovate, and white flowers cluster at the top of the branches. Sow the seeds under glass in March and transplant out of doors in May, 20 cm apart, or keep it indoors as a pot herb where it will survive well into winter.

The ancient Greeks believed Basil represented hate and misfortune and that the plant would not grow unless abused, whereas in India it has always been cherished as a holy plant. When a Hindu equivalent for the Bible has been needed in British courts, Basil has been deemed holy enough to use. It has a mild flavour when compared with Sweet Basil, but the leaves are used in a similar way for seasoning and in salads.

Ocimum minimum photographed 3 August

Sweet Basil photographed 3 August

Sweet Basil

Ocimum basilicum, an annual originating in India, grows in a frost-free climate. It has shiny green leaves, with whorls of white blooms on the upper stem. It grows to 50 cm. A popular hybrid, **Purple Basil**, has dark purple-bronze leaves with pink flowers. It is best grown from seed in a light rich soil or compost under glass, and transplanted to a sunny position, 20 cm apart. When the plants are established pinch out the centre buds to encourage bushy growth.

Dishes such as soupe au pistou of the Nice district and pesto sauce of Genoa depend entirely on fresh leaves of Basil for their existence. It is wonderful eaten with tomatoes. The powerful, aromatic flavour is superb mixed in green salads, scattered over egg dishes or added, with garlic, to cooked mushrooms. Basil looses its pungent flavour when dried.

Ocimum basilicum with leaves from the purple hybrid photographed 3 August

Hyssop photographed 14 August

Hyssop

Hyssopus officinalis is a hardy perennial from Southern Europe and Russia. It grows to 60 cm. Its royal blue, white or pink flowers bloom from June to September. Sow seeds in moist soil in April and thin the plants to 60 cm apart, or take cuttings in spring or autumn. Hyssop grows well in containers.

A common garden plant, it is cultivated as an aromatic and medicinal herb. It has a slightly bitter and minty taste and was popular for cooking in the Middle Ages, when chopped leaves were substituted for parsley and chervil to give a tang to soups and roast meats. Its chief use is as a remedy for all respiratory complaints. Hyssop tea made with the flowers is an expectorant and eases tightness of the chest; or it can be made into a syrup to relieve coughs by adding sugar and re-heating. This must be taken in small amounts because it can act as an irritant.

Hyssopus officinalis photographed 14 August

Rosemary photographed 16 May

Rosemary

Rosmarinus officinalis is an evergreen herb from the Mediterranean coast. It grows to 2 metres and flowers in the spring or summer. It is best grown from cuttings taken in August, put into light sandy soil and transplanted out of doors the following spring in a sunny position.

There is an old saying, 'rosemary for remembrance' which may have arisen from when the Greeks and Romans wore crowns made from the plant to enliven their minds and improve their memory. It is a strongly aromatic herb with a slightly camphoric taste, and is used to flavour roast lamb and kid. In Italy the herb is so popular that butchers give away sprigs of it with the meat. Try adding it to chicken or rabbit dishes which are cooked with wine and garlic. The flavour also blends well with fish, especially halibut. It can be used in sweet recipes: jams, jellies and fruit salads.

Rosmarinus officinalis photographed 16 May

Curly Leaved Parsley photographed 5 June

Curly Leaved Parsley

Petroselinum crispum is a biennial from the Mediterranean region. It grows to 60 cm and flowers during the summer. Curly-leaved Parsley is the most popular variety grown in Britain whereas **French** or **Plain-leaved Parsley**, which is far hardier, is preferred on the Continent. The seeds take up to four weeks to germinate but this period can be reduced if they are pre-soaked in luke-warm water prior to planting in a rich, moist soil. For a continuous supply of this herb sow in February, May and August.

This refreshing, slightly sweet herb is used as a garnish on most savoury dishes. It is rich in vitamin C and should be eaten daily, scattered over vegetables and soups, mixed in salads or added to sauces to accompany fish. Two other varieties of parsley, Neapolitan, grown for the stems, and Hamburg, grown for its root, are both cultivated in Italy and served as vegetables.

Petroselinum crispum photographed 15 July

Fennel, *Foeniculum vulgare* photographed 17 July

Fennel

Foeniculum vulgare, a perennial from southern Europe, is common in the south of England and Wales on waste places and around the coast. It grows to 1.4 metres and flowers from July to October. The bright green feathery leaves contrast with the popular hybrid, **Bronze Fennel**, which has purple-tinged fronds. Sow the seeds in moist, well-drained soil during the spring. Thin plants to 30 cm. Fennel has a sweet aniseed flavour which is superb with fish, either added to sauces or stuffings or as a garnish. The leaves are a basic ingredient of 'grillade au fenouil', and red mullet, barbecued on a bed of fennel, is another French speciality.

Florence Fennel, *Foeniculum vulgare* var. *azoricum*, is a variety which has an edible, swollen leaf base similar to celery. It grows to 30 cm. It can be cultivated like common fennel but it does need a long, warm growing season to mature. The bulbous root is a popular cooked vegetable in Italy and it is delicious added to salads.

Florence Fennel, *Foeniculum dulce* photographed 14 August

Lovage photographed 29 May

Lovage

Levisticum officinale is a perennial from southern Europe. It grows to 2 metres and flowers from June to July. Propagate by root division in spring or sow the seeds in rich, well-drained soil in a sunny position in autumn. Thin seedlings to 30 cm apart. It is sometimes grown in gardens for its ornamental foliage.

It was originally a popular culinary and medicinal herb used by the Greeks and Romans, and cultivated in Britain, but it is little known today. The whole plant is edible, emitting when bruised an aromatic scent similar to Celery. The leaves have a strong flavour so add sparingly to soups, casseroles, salads and omelettes. The young stems may be candied and used to decorate cakes, the seeds can be baked in bread or cheese biscuits, and the fleshy root cooked and served as a vegetable. Lovage was used as a 'bath herb' because it has a cleansing and deodorizing effect on the skin.

Levisticum officinalis photographed 14 July

Coriander photographed 5 July

Coriander

Coriandrum sativum, an annual from southern Europe, is found wild in Britain as a garden escape. It grows to 80 cm and flowers from June throughout the summer. Sow the seeds in early spring in a light, rich soil in a sunny position. Harvest the plant in August when the fruit has turned from green to grey. Leave the seeds on the plant for a few days before drying.

Coriander is an ancient spice and was used to preserve meats and flavour unpleasant medicines. It is grown mainly for its seeds but the young leaves add a clean, refreshing tang to soups and salads. The mild spicy seeds are an essential ingredient for curries, and in India they roast and then grind them to enhance their curry-like taste. An excellent spice in stuffings, sweet-sour pickles and chutneys. The flavour of Coriander combines well with cooked beetroot, celery and cauliflower.

Coriandrum sativum photographed 5 July

Wild Celery photographed 28 June

Celery

Celery, *Apium graveolens*, is found as a wild plant in wet places, usually along tidal rivers or near the sea, throughout Britain and much of Europe, Asia and America. It is a perennial, and the greenish flowers appear in stalkless umbels throughout the summer. It is very pungent, and in its wild form does not seem to have been much used.

Cultivated Celery, in which the swollen leaf stalks are commonly eaten, is a less pungent variety (var. *dulce*) and **Celeriac**, var. *rapaceum*, is a variety in which the base of the stem becomes swollen.

The closely-related **Fool's Watercress**, *Apium nodiflorum*, is a creeping plant found inland along streams, commonly growing among watercress. It may be used sparingly as a flavouring in soups and stews, but be careful not to confuse it with young leaves of the very poisonous **Hemlock Water Dropwort**, *Oenanthe crocata*, a larger plant with Celery-like leaves.

Apium graveolens photographed 28 June

Caraway photographed 16 July

Caraway

Carum carvi, a biennial, grows wild in Europe and parts of Asia. It grows to 60 cm and flowers from June to July. Seeds sown in autumn will produce a crop by next summer. Plant in well-drained soil in a sunny position. Remove seed heads when the fruit turns brown and dry. Scatter seeds over breads or bake in cakes and biscuits. The spice is used to flavour cheese and sauerkraute. The root is eaten as a vegetable and the young leaves added to salads.

Anise, *Pimpinella anisum*, is an annual from Egypt which grows to 45 cm and only flowers in hot summers. Sow the seeds in April in light, well-drained soil. Anise tastes similar to liquorice and is best known for flavouring drinks such as Pernod, Anisette and Greek Ouzo. Add the seeds to biscuits, cakes, breads and apple pies. Seeds eaten after a meal sweeten the breath and aid digestion. The chopped leaves can be used as a seasoning for vegetables, soups and stews.

Carum carvi photographed 16 July

Sweet Cecily seeds photographed 5 August

Sweet Cecily

Myrrhis odorata, a perennial, probably native, is found in northern England and southern Scotland in grassy places, hedges and wood edges. It grows to 1 metre and flowers from April to July. Sow the seeds in spring, in moist soil in partial shade where plants are to blossom. The flowers should be cut off to retain the flavour in the leaves.

A fragrant plant with a sweet aniseed flavour, it is used as a sweetening herb. Finely chopped leaves added to rhubarb, gooseberries or other tart fruits help to reduce the acidity and cut down the amount of sugar needed, which is ideal for diabetics and people trying to lose weight. The leaves can be used to season soups and stews or mixed into salads. The roots are boiled, dressed in oil and vinegar and eaten cold. As a cure for indigestion either chew the ripe seeds or drink Sweet Cecily tea.

Myrrhis odorata photographed 14 July

Dill photographed 9 June

Dill

Anethum graveolens is a hardy annual from southern Europe which grows to 80 cm. The small umbels of yellow flowers blossom from June to August. Sow the seeds in late spring in a sunny position where the plants are to flower. Thin seedlings to 30 cm apart.

The aromatic leaves taste sweet whilst the seeds are bitter. Dill is a popular culinary herb in Scandinavia where it is added to sauces and served with fish as an alternative to Fennel. It is a common ingredient used for pickling, especially cucumber, known as dill pickles. The flavour tends to 'cook away' so add the herb just before serving. Sprinkle chopped leaves over potatoes and green salads or combine with cucumber and yoghurt. Medicinally it has a calming effect and gripe water, made from the seeds, is given to babies to stop hiccups and induce sleep.

Anethum graveolens photographed 9 June

Chervil photographed 20 May

Chervil

Anthriscus cerefolium is a biannual from southeast Europe. It grows to 45 cm and flowers in June. Sow seeds in spring in well-drained soil in partial shade. Thin plants to 15 cm. Seeds germinate quickly so with successive sowing it is possible to have fresh leaves almost all year round. Can be grown in window boxes.

The herb has a delicate taste and should be used fresh. Chervil soup is delicious but to retain its flavour add the leaves just before serving. Add to butter sauces and serve with fish or vegetables, scatter a few sprigs over green salads, combine in egg recipes or use as a garnish for pork and veal dishes. Chervil is one of the traditional herbs used in 'Fines herbes' and bouquet garnis. In France it is so popular it is used instead of parsley.

Anthriscus cerefolium photographed 26 June

Tansy photographed 19 August

Tansy

Tanacetum vulgare, a perennial common throughout Britain is found in hedgerows, roadsides and waste places. It grows to 1 metre and flowers from July to September. It flourishes in almost any soil and is propagated by root division or can be grown from seed.

Tansy was a commonly used cottage garden herb in medieval times, customarily eaten at Easter to purify the blood after the Lenten fast. The leaves were mixed into a pudding, 'tansies', made with milk, eggs and flour and although Gerard, the 17th century herbalist, claims it to be 'pleasant in taste and good for the stomach . . .' it is not to be recommended. Freshly chopped young leaves can be eaten with fried or scrambled eggs. The repugnant odour acts as a repellent and the plant was traditionally rubbed onto meat to keep off bluebottles, and on corpses to save them from earthworms.

Tanacetum vulgare photographed 19 August

Tarragon photographed 26 June

French Tarragon

Artemisia dracunculus is a perennial from Siberia. It grows to 1 metre and only flowers in warm climates from May to June. **Russian Tarragon** has rough green leaves, is taller and lacks the tartness of French or True Tarragon which has smooth green foliage. It can be grown from cuttings or root division. Plant during spring in well-drained soil, in a sunny position, 45 cm apart. Cut down plants in winter and cover with straw to protect against frost. Renew beds every four years.

This herb is the main flavouring in sauce bearnaise and sauce tartare. It enhances the flavour of lobster and is added to stuffings for meat and roast chicken. Make tarragon vinegar by filling a bottle with the fresh leaves and covering them with white wine vinegar. After two months it is ready to use in salad dressings or mayonnaise.

Artemisia dracunculus photographed 26 June

Horseradish photographed 12 May

Horseradish

Armoracia rusticana, a perennial from eastern Europe, is found in southern England on roadsides and banks. It grows to 90 cm and flowers from May to June. Grow from seed or pieces of root, planted 5 cm deep in a sunny position in early spring.

Horseradish root is used raw because it loses its pungency when cooked. It is mainly used as a condiment, grated into cream and mixed with a dash of white wine vinegar and a spoonful of sugar. Traditionally this sauce is served with roast beef but it is delicious with smoked mackerel or herring. The roots should be dug up in the autumn and stored in damp sand until required. Grating Horseradish makes your eyes smart and is tear-inducing. Medicinally, the root is applied to chilblains to relieve the pain. The juice, mixed with vinegar, is supposed to remove freckles.

Armoracia rusticana photographed 14 September

Borage photographed 19 June

Borage

Borago officinalis, an annual from the Middle East, is found as a garden escape on waste places. It grows to 50 cm and flowers from June to September. Sow seeds 5 cm deep, in light, well-drained soil from early spring. Plants are fully grown in six weeks.

People used to eat Borage because they believed it acted as a tonic, inducing a state of euphoria. The young leaves, which taste of cucumber, are added to salads but they must be shredded finely because their bristly texture makes them unappetizing when whole. They also taste superb mixed with yoghurt or cottage cheese. The flowers are edible and make an attractive garnish on salads or they can be candied and used to decorate cakes and desserts. The herb is commonly used to flavour summer drinks, especially Pimm's or home-made lemonade.

Borago officinalis photographed 19 June

Saffron Crocus photographed 23 September

Saffron

Crocus sativus, a perennial corm, originates from Asia Minor. It grows to 20 cm and flowers in September. Plant the corms in a rich, sandy but well-drained soil, 15 cm apart, in August. They can be grown from seed but you have to wait three years for them to flower.

Saffron is cultivated for the orange-red stigmas. It was grown extensively at Saffron Walden in Essex but the finest supplies now come from Spain. It is expensive because at least 60,000 flowers are needed to make one pound of saffron. The flowers are gathered in September and the stigmas are picked out and kiln dried. This herb has a spicy, aromatic and slightly bitter taste. Only a tiny amount is needed to give colour and flavour. Add to the Provençal dish, Bouillabaisse, and other fish soups, stews and paellas. It is a basic ingredient in risotto milanese.

Crocus sativus photographed 23 September

Bay photographed 10 August

Bay

Laurus nobilis, a small shrubby tree, is a native of Mediterranean countries and grows to 12 metres. It needs a warm climate to produce flowers and berries. Trees should be planted in spring or autumn. Ideal for growing in pots, filled with equal portions of sand, loam and peat and covered with manure.

The plant has a double role which is aptly described by Doctor Lecterc, it 'crowns the heads of heroes and flavours the stews of plebs'. Bay was the ceremonial laurel of the ancient Greeks and Romans, symbolizing wisdom and glory, and also supposedly protecting them against lightning. Laurel crowns were worn by emperors, warriors and poets. Bay is one of the three herbs in bouquet garni. Its aromatic leaves are an essential ingredient for flavouring soups, sauces, court-bouillons and marinades. The leaves are placed in boxes of dried figs and liquorice to keep out weevils.

Laurus nobilis photographed 10 August

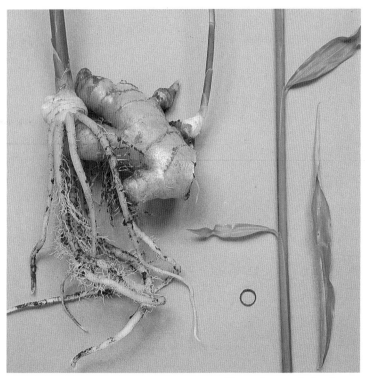

Ginger photographed 10 August

Fenugreek

Trigonella foenum-graecum is a hardy annual from Western Asia. It grows to 60 cm and flowers from June to August. The seeds should be sown in well-drained soil; they take four months to mature. Then the plant should be up-rooted and dried. Alternatively, they can be grown like bean sprouts. The ground seeds are a basic ingredient in curry powders and the Jewish sweet dish, Halva. The young shoots are chopped and added to salads or in India the bitter leaves are eaten as a vegetable.

Ginger

Zingiber officinale is a perennial from southeast Asia. It grows to 75 cm. Its flowers are yellow with a purple lip and it can only be grown in tropical climates. Fresh ginger roots, referred to as 'hands', taste milder than the dried variety and should be peeled, ground to a pulp and used in curries. To make ginger powder, grind the dried root in an electric mill and use it to flavour biscuits and cakes or serve as a condiment with melon and peaches.

Fenugreek photographed 17 July

Chicory photographed 17 July

Chicory or Wild Succory

Cichovium intybus, a perennial herb, usually cultivated as an annual, is native to Europe and is common in southern England. It grows to 1.2 metres and flowers from July to October. Sow the seeds in June. For the forced white leaf crowns, dig up the roots in October, remove the leaves and replant in a warm green-house in boxes half filled with sand, and cover to exclude the light. Roots taken for roasting should be lifted at the same time.

Blanched Chicory is also referred to as **Endive** or **Witloaf**. The crisp white leaves add a sharp edge to winter salads, or they are delicious cooked as a vegetable and served with a cream sauce with roast meat or game. The unblanched plant is bitter and the roasted, ground roots are a well-known flavouring for coffee, especially on the Continent: the French believe that it counteracts the effect of caffeine.

Cichovium intybus photographed 4 April

Marigolds photographed 4 July

Marigold

Calendula officinalis is an annual from southern Europe and Asia. It grows to 40 cm and flowers from June until the first frost. Sow seeds in any soil in a sunny position, during spring. If the plants go to seed they will freely self-sow.

This popular garden plant only opens its flowers during the day. German fables claim that it is a sign of rain if the flowers remain closed after seven o'clock in the morning. Marigold petals can be used as a substitute for saffron to colour rice but they have a different flavour. They are also used as a colouring agent for cakes, by pre-soaking the petals in warm milk before adding to the other ingredients. They make an unusual garnish scattered over green salads or fruit desserts. The young leaves can be eaten but they are tough and have a bitter, salty taste.

Calendula officinalis photographed 4 July

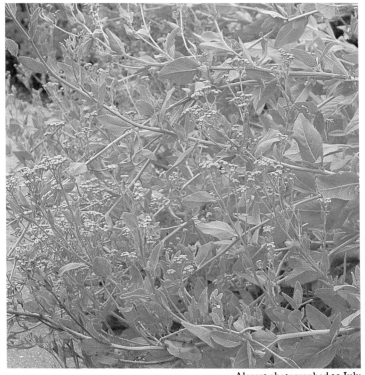

Alecost photographed 29 July

Costmary or Alecost

Chrysanthemum balsamita is a hardy perennial from the Orient. A popular herb in the 16th century which, as Gerard noted, 'groweth everywhere in gardens', but it has since gone out of fashion and is now a rarity, occasionally found in Lincolnshire where it is known as **Mace**. It grows to 80 cm and flowers from June to July. Propagate by root division in spring or autumn and plant in a dry, sheltered position. The creeping roots spread quickly. Thin every third year.

Alecost, with its aromatic, spicy leaves was employed to flavour home-brewed ale. Another name ascribed to it, **Bibleleaf**, originated from when early American colonists put the long leaves into their Bibles and used them as book-markers. The fresh leaves were eaten in salads and potages or were dried and used medicinally to calm upset stomachs. Costmary is added to pot pourri to intensify the scent of other plants.

Chrysanthemum balsamita photographed 29 July

Dandelions photographed 3 May

Dandelion
Taraxacum officinale is a perennial, common throughout Britain in road-side verges, meadows and as a garden weed. It grows to 35 cm and flowers open only in full sun from March to September. If you wish to grow a crop of dandelions propagate from seed or root division.

A cleansing herb, rich in vitamins and minerals, it acts as a diuretic and was known as 'Piss-a-bed'. Perhaps this explains how the famous French salad, Pissenlit, comprising chopped young leaves, squares of crispy fried bacon and croutons tossed in a light dressing, got its name. The leaves can be blanched or used green in salads or cooked as a vegetable like spinach. The flower heads are gathered to make wine, which tastes similar to the Greek Retsina. The roots, dug in autumn, are dried, roasted, then ground and used as a substitute for coffee.

Taraxacum officinale photographed 3 May

Shepherd's Purse photographed 4 April

Shepherd's Purse

Capsella bursa-pastoris is an annual, abundant throughout the British Isles in waste places and as a garden weed. It grows to 35 cm and flowers all year. The plant was named after its flat seed-pouches which resemble old-fashioned leather purses. It is also called **Mother's Heart**.

The leaves, which taste similar to cress, are delicious in sandwiches or added to salads. The fresh or dried herb infused in boiling water and drunk as a tea is considered by herbalists to be an excellent cure for stopping all kinds of haemorrhages and regularizing menstruation. A wad of cotton wool soaked in the infusion and then inserted into the nostril stops nose-bleeds.

Capsella bursa-pastoris photographed 4 April

Angelica photographed 23 July

Angelica

Angelica archangelica, a perennial from Syria, now naturalized in northern Europe, is found in damp shady places. It grows to 2 metres and flowers from July to August. Sow the seed in late summer out-of-doors and it will flower in its second or third year.

Angelica is best known for the candied, young green stems used to decorate cakes and trifles, but all parts of the plant have a use. Blanch the shoots and mix into a salad or add the leaf stalks to jam or rhubarb for a musky flavour. Syrup can be made from the leaves and the stems and roots can be eaten as a vegetable. The seeds are used in the preparation of Vermouth and Chartreuse. A tea made from the leaves calms the nerves, relieves colds, coughs and rheumatism but should not be drunk by diabetics. Angelica is considered to be on a par with Ginseng: an elixir of long life.

Angelica archangelica photographed 23 July

Skirret photographed 10 July

Skirret

Sium sisarum, a hardy perennial from China, is cultivated in Europe. It is usually grown as an annual for its roots which are eaten as a vegetable. It grows to 1.2 metres and flowers from June to August. Propagate by taking off the side roots just before new growth appears or sow the seeds during April in a light, rich soil. When the seedlings are large enough thin to 20 cm apart.

The roots may be harvested from the end of September onwards. Skirret, similar to Salsify, is boiled and eaten as a vegetable with melted butter or sliced into slivers, tossed in a vinaigrette, scattered with parsley, chilled and served as a salad. Like parsnip, the sweet white roots can be roasted or made into soup. Seventeenth century herbalist Culpepper claims that it acts as a diuretic and cleansing herb, and it is reputed to be a beneficial ingredient in alleviating chest complaints.

Sium sisarum photographed 10 July

Common Sorrel photographed 27 May

Common Sorrel

Rumex acetosa, a hardy perennial from Europe, is found in meadows and along roadsides throughout the British Isles. It grows to 60 cm and flowers from May to July. It has arrow-shaped lobes at the base of the leaves whereas **French Sorrel**, considered by some as superior for cooking, has broad, shield-shaped leaves. Propagate by root division or sow seeds in spring in a sunny position. Renew plants every four years because they tend to get woody and tough. Sorrels are sour docks. The name originates from an old Teutonic word for 'sour'. The young leaves are used to season omelettes, salads, lamb and beef stews. They can be cooked as a vegetable but not in an iron pan because they will acquire a metallic taste. Sorrel soup is delicious. The sour flavour is excellent for making sauces to serve with fish, especially salmon. Sorrel tea is reputed to relieve kidney and liver disorders.

Rumex acetosa photographed 27 May

Bistort photographed 11 May

Bistort

Polygonum bistorta, a perennial, native of northern Europe, is common on roadsides and meadows in the north of England. It grows to 20 cm and flowers from May to August. Propagate by root division or grow from seed.

The name bistorta comes from the Latin, bis, meaning twice and torta, twisted, which probably refers to the plants' contorted rhizome which resembles a coiled snake and helps explain its local names, **Adderwort** and **Snakeweed**. In the Lake District it is known as **Easter Ledge** because the young leaves with nettles, onion, boiled barley and an egg are made into Easter Ledger pudding and eaten with bacon at the end of the Lenten fast. It is believed to be a good spring tonic. The roots are used as a powerful astringent. Twenty-five grams of the bruised root boiled in one pint of water taken in doses of a tablespoon every two hours is a remedy for diarrhoea, colic and haemorrhages.

Polygonum bistorta photographed 11 May

Nasturtiums photographed 14 July

Nasturtium

Tropaeolum majus, an annual from Peru, is a common creeping and climbing plant grown in gardens all over the world. Sow the seeds in spring in light sandy soil in a sunny position. Once established they seed themselves prolifically. They grow well in window boxes and flower from June to October.

Nasturtiums were eaten as a remedy against scurvy because of their high vitamin C and iron content. The fresh leaves and flowers look attractive in salads and their strong peppery, watercress taste provides a valuable alternative seasoning for people on a salt-free diet. The chopped leaves are ideal for flavouring cream cheese dips and in sandwiches. The young buds and green seeds, pickled in wine vinegar for a month, can be used as a substitute for capers. Medicinally the herb is used as a tonic to cleanse the blood and digestive organs.

Tropaeolum majus photographed 14 July

Green Purslane photographed 5 June

Green Purslane

Portulaca oleracea, an annual, native of many regions of Europe, is a sprawling, succulent plant. It grows to 15 cm, and flowers from June to July. A popular variety, **Golden Purslane**, has yellow leaves instead of green, and is not so hardy. Sow the seeds in a sandy soil in a sunny position from April. The leaves will be ready to pick in 6 or 7 weeks. Sow monthly to give a continuous supply.

Traditionally, purslane was eaten to prevent scurvy because it is rich in vitamins, minerals and trace elements. The young leaves should be picked as required and used fresh in green salads. The shoots, tied into bundles of equal length, can be cooked like asparagus and served with melted butter. The thick stems and fleshy leaves can be pickled in salt and vinegar and used in winter salads. Purslane tea is a tonic and clears blood disorders.

Portulaca oleracea photographed 14 July

Salad Burnet photographed 7 May

Salad Burnet

Sanguisorba minor, a perennial, native of Europe, is found on chalk downs in southern England. It grows to 30 cm and flowers from May to August. Sow the seeds in spring or autumn in light soil. For a plentiful supply of tender young leaves keep flower heads cut back. The cucumber-flavoured leaves are excellent in salads or blended with cream cheese for a dip or used as a garnish. It can be used in herb butters and is one of the basic ingredients for ravigote and chivry sauces. Add to wine cups and cooling summer drinks.

Greater Burnet, *Sanguisorba officinalis*, is a native perennial found in damp meadows in northern England. It grows to 70 cm and flowers from June to September. Sow the seeds in April. Use in a similar way to Salad Burnet. Burnet comes from the Old French 'Burnette' and refers to the mahogany flowers. Medicinally, like its relative, it was used to staunch the blood.

86

Left to right, Salad Burnet; Greater Burnet photographed 10 June

Garlic photographed 27 July

Garlic

Allium sativum, a perennial from Asia, is cultivated in warm climates throughout the world. It grows to 60 cm and flowers from June to July. Garlic flourishes in rich, well-drained soil in a sunny position. Break the bulbs into cloves and plant 5 cm deep in February. Lift in the autumn when the tops have died down and dry under cover.

Garlic acts as a tonic, aids digestion, reduces blood pressure, clears bronchitis and staves off colds and headaches. In Sweden cloves were attached to the necks of animals to protect them from trolls or to prevent goblins stealing milk from the cows. Add abundantly to most savoury dishes: cook in stews, soups, with vegetables and put into salad dressings or make Aiole, the French garlic sauce. For a mild flavour just rub the cooking vessel with garlic.

Allium satirum photographed 3 August

Chives photographed 2 June

Chives

Allium schoenoprasum, a native perennial bulb, is occasionally found in limestone regions. It grows to 30 cm. The pale mauve flowers bloom from June to July and should be cut off to keep the flavour in the leaves. Chives can be grown from seed but they are usually propagated by dividing the clumps in spring or autumn and planting in a light, rich, damp soil. They grow well in containers but need a liquid feed every 14 days.

The delicate onion flavour of chives is superb for garnishing all salads and vegetable soups. The taste combines well with omelettes and scrambled eggs. Added to cream cheese or butter it makes an excellent sandwich-filling or topping for baked potatoes. Relatives of the Chive, the Welsh Onion and Spring Onion, are stronger in growth and piquancy, making them ideal for cooking especially in stir-fry recipes, but they can also be used raw in salads.

Allium schoenoprasum photographed 14 June

Lawn Chamomile photographed 28 July

Double-centred Chamomile

Chamomilla recutita, a native annual, is common in arable fields, along road verges and on waste places in southern England. It grows to 50 cm and flowers from May to August, the petals turning back to bare the dense yellow centres. They are picked just before they are in full bloom, dried and used to make tisanes. Chamomile tea, made with 1–2 teaspoons of dried flowers in a cup of boiling water, is drunk as a tonic and to relieve stomach pains, cystitis and rheumatism. An infusion is used as a gargle for toothache or as an eyebath and it is an excellent herbal hair rinse for blonds. Sow the seeds during the spring.

Lawn Chamomile, *Anthemis nobilis*, a perennial, has double-centred white flowers which blossom from May to August. It is grown as a herb lawn because of the beautiful sweet smell that the blooms exude when crushed. Scatter the seeds during the spring.

Wild Chamomile photographed 17 June

Coltsfoot photographed 29 March

Coltsfoot

Tussilago farfara, a native perennial, is found in abundance on banks, waste places and in poor soil. It grows to 25 cm. The flowers appear before the leaves, in March to April. They then give way to a ball of down and the seeds are dispersed by the wind. This attractive weed is not generally cultivated.

In Paris the flowers of this medicinal herb were painted on the door-posts of apothecary shops. The Latin word for cough is *tussis* which could explain why this plant is used as a remedy for coughs. Coltsfoot tea, sweetened with honey, stops coughing and soothes sore throats. The leaves are the basis for herbal tobaccos, smoked to relieve asthma and to aid difficult breathing caused by bronchitis, without any of the injurious effects of ordinary tobacco. The leaves, rich in vitamin C, can be added to salads and a light, refreshing wine can be made with the flowers.

Tussilago farfara photographed 29 March

Yarrow photographed 23 August

Yarrow or Milfoil

Achillea millefolium, native perennial, is found on roadsides, meadows and as a garden weed throughout Britain. It grows to 45 cm and flowers from June to November. Yarrow is easily transplanted and will grow in any soil. The roots secrete a beneficial substance which helps neighbouring plants to resist disease and it seems to intensify the aroma of nearby herbs.

Yarrow, highly prized as a wound herb, was first used by Achilles to cleanse and heal his companions' wounds. A tea made with the flowers and leaves is a general fortifier. It relieves intestinal troubles, regulates menstrual periods and acts as a diuretic which aids the functions of the liver, gall bladder and kidneys. Chewing the fresh leaves is reputed to cure toothache. An infusion of the flowers makes a good lotion for cleansing the skin and added to bath water has a relaxing effect.

Achillea millefolium photographed 23 August

Wormwood photographed 10 August

Wormwood

Artemisa absinthium, a native perennial, is found on waste places and roadsides. It grows to 80 cm and flowers from July to August. Sow the seeds in a shady position in autumn or propagate by root division or from cuttings.

In France people used to scour the countryside looking for Wormwood to dig up the root and make Absinthe, until its manufacture was banned in 1915. Excessive drinking of this alcoholic liquor was deadly, causing hallucinations and permanent brain damage.

In spite of its lethal association with Absinthe, Wormwood is a valuable medicinal herb for stimulating the appetite and aiding digestion. Tea made from the leaves and flowers is a tonic, diuretic and laxative and powdered flowers are taken to expel worms. This aromatic plant was hung indoors to rid houses of fleas and insects and put amongst clothes to keep away moths.

Artemisa absinthium photographed 10 August

Lemon Balm photographed 24 June

Lemon Balm

Melissa officinalis, a perennial from southern Europe, is found as a garden escape in Britain. It grows to 60 cm and flowers from June to October. Cultivate by root division or take cuttings and plant in a sunny position in spring or autumn. It can be grown from seed but they take a long time to germinate.

Bees are attracted to Lemon Balm which is indicated by its botanical name, Melissa, the Greek word for bee. The essence of balm mixed with wine was taken to rejuvenate the mind. The delicate lemon flavour is used to season stuffings for lamb or pork and is an ideal ingredient for marinades and herb sauces to serve with fish. Added to stewed fruits, jams and jellies it acts as a substitute for lemon, and the young leaves give a refreshing tang to summer drinks. Lemon Balm tea is reputed to be a tonic and drunk to alleviate fevers. The sweet-scented leaves make it an ideal plant to add to pot-pourri.

Melissa officinalis photographed 24 June

Wild Bergamot photographed 29 July

Bergamot

Monarda didyma is a perennial from North America which grows to 60 cm and flowers in mid-summer. The pale green, hairy leaves and bright scarlet flowers differ from **Wild Bergamot** which has pinkish blooms and smooth foliage. Propagate by taking cuttings or by root division and plant in a rich, moist soil in partial shade in spring or autumn. It should be dug up every two years to remove the old, woody roots.

Bergamot is sometimes called **Oswego Tea**, named after the Oswego Indians who first used the leaves to make a fragrant beverage. At the Boston Tea Party, colonists drank this tea as a protest against British imports. It is now drunk in the United States for its relaxing effect. The plant is also known as **Bee Balm** as bees are fond of the aromatic blossoms. The chopped leaves and petals look attractive scattered over green or fresh fruit salads.

Monarda didyma

Elder photographed 18 September

Elder

Sambucus nigra, a native shrub, flourishes in woods, hedgerows and waste places throughout Britain. It grows to 7 metres. It is claimed that our English summer is not here until the Elder is in full flower in June and ends when the berries are ripe in September.

The stems and leaves stink when bruised but the blossom has a sweet scent. The flowers may be eaten as fritters, coated in batter and deep fried. They add a superb flavour to cooked fruits, especially gooseberries. Elderflower champagne is easy to make and ready to drink within three weeks. Serve chilled with a sprig of mint. The wine should be drunk during the winter as its sweet fragrance and taste is so evocative of long, warm, summer days. Elderberry wine, rich in tannin, takes several years to mature and can taste similar to port.

Elder flowers photographed 21 June

Pleached Lime Trees photographed 15 June

Lime or Linden

Tilia europaea, a large deciduous tree, is native to Europe, and can be found throughout Britain in woods, parkland, hedgerows, gardens and planted in long avenues, lining drive-ways. It grows to 25 metres and flowers from June to July.

The yellowish flowers grow in clusters of four or more and have long, wing-shaped bracts attached to the stalks. Honey from the flowers is highly esteemed for its sweet, distinctive flavour and is very expensive. It is used medicinally and to sweeten liqueurs. Linden tea, a common drink on the Continent, is made from the dried flowers. Allow one teaspoon per cup and one for the pot and leave to steep for several minutes before pouring. It has a slightly aromatic taste and can be drunk hot or cold. This tea aids the digestion, calms the nerves and is said to induce sleep if taken before going to bed.

Lime flowers photographed 15 June

Juniper tree photographed 20 April

Juniper
Juniperus communis is a small evergreen tree, and is common throughout the northern hemisphere, where it can be found on chalk downs and heaths in southern England and on bands of limestone in the Lake District and Scotland. It grows to 4 metres and flowers in May and June. The berries appear on female trees in September but take three years to ripen, changing from green to blue and finally turning black.

The berries are best known for their use in flavouring gin but their aromatic and pungent flavour, slightly reminiscent of pine, is also excellent for cooking. Traditionally they were added to dry-spice mixtures and brine for curing beef, ham and salt pork. They are a wonderful seasoning for patés and stuffings for game or they can be put into marinades for venison and mutton. A conserve made from the berries is served as a condiment with cold meat.

Juniper berries photographed 20 April

May Apple photographed 11 May

May Apple or American Mandrake

Podophyllum peltatum (Berberis family) is a common plant of damp woods in eastern North America. It forms large patches by means of creeping underground stems, and the small white flowers which appear in spring are usually hidden beneath the developing leaves. The fruits (shown here immature) are yellow or red when ripe, and sweet, and more or less edible.

The juice of the stems and rhizomes, however, is very poisonous and can be fatal. It has been found to be useful medicinally in the treatment of venereal warts and other skin cancers, on which it works by inhibiting cell division. It is too poisonous to be used internally.

Some other species of *Podophyllum* are found in the Himalayas and China, and one, *P. emodi*, is commonly grown in gardens for its beautiful pink flowers.

Podophyllum peltatum photographed 11 May

Lesser Celandine photographed 23 March

Greater Celandine
Chelidonium majus, a perennial, possibly native, is found on banks and
hedgerows in England. It grows to 75 cm and flowers from May to July.
Chelidonium is the Greek word for swallow and when the flowers bloom it
indicates their arrival. The plant contains poisonous substances and must
not be taken internally. The orange juice from the stem has been used to
cure warts and ringworm but must only be applied to the affected area.
Lesser Celandine, *Ranunculus ficaria*, a native perennial, is abundant in
woods, meadows and stream-sides in the British Isles. It grows to 20 cm
and flowers from March to May. Wordsworth's favourite flower, its
blossoms are carved on his tomb. An ointment can be made by adding the
bruised herb to some fresh lard, or an infusion to drink made by steeping
the roots in boiling water or wine: these are both effective cures for piles
hence its local name, **Pilewort**.

Greater Celandine photographed 14 June

Opium Poppy photographed 14 July

Opium Poppy
Papaver somniferum, an annual from Asia Minor, is occasionally found in Britain as a garden escape. It grows to 60 cm and flowers from June to August. Sow the seeds in a rich moist soil in a sunny position during March. The seeds are ready to harvest in September.

Somniferum means sleep-bearing in Latin. The drug, Opium, comes from the white-flowered subspecies and for this reason in Britain and America you need a licence to grow this plant. The drug, a juice rich in morphine and codeine alkaloids, is extracted from the flower heads just after the petals have fallen. However, the seeds when ripe, have lost all traces of the drug and are widely used in Jewish confectionery, sprinkled onto bread, biscuits and cakes. The hard seeds are difficult to grind or crush but if successful you can add them to curry dishes and their nutty flavour gives interest to milk puddings.

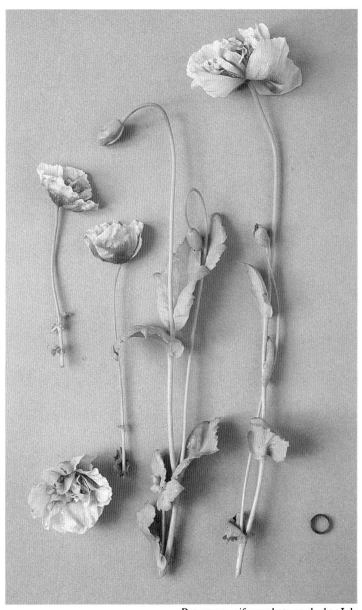

Papaver somniferum photographed 14 July

Rue photographed 3 August

Rue

Ruta graveolens, an evergreen perennial from southern Europe, was introduced to Britain by the Romans. It grows to 50 cm and flowers from June to September. Sow seeds outside in spring, and when 5 cm high transplant into fresh beds, 45 cm apart. The plant thrives in poor soil but prefers a sheltered position.

Shakespeare called Rue the 'Herb of Grace'. It was used for relieving indigestion and easing eye strain, and poultices made from the juice of the leaves, were used to draw out poison from serpent bites or bee stings. In small doses, a leaf or two, it acts as a stimulant but some people are allergic to it and large quantities are dangerous. It has a strong aromatic scent with a pungent, acrid taste and tiny amounts can be used in salads or to flavour fish or egg dishes. In Italy, sprigs of Rue are added to Grappa, a distilled grape spirit.

Rue with leaves from a variegated hybrid photographed 3 August

Ground Elder photographed 10 June

Goutweed or Ground Elder

Aegopodium podagraria, a perennial, is rampant throughout the British Isles along road verges, in waste places and as a garden weed. It grows to 90 cm and flowers from May to July.

Goutweed was introduced into Britain during the Middle Ages as a pot herb and was used medicinally to heal gout. Its leaves, similar to Elder, explain why the plant is also known as **Ground Elder**, **Dog** or **Dwarf Elder**. The young leaves, picked in spring and cooked like spinach, then tossed in butter, are a delicious vegetable. They can also be eaten raw in salads. Homeopathic doctors prescribe this herb to soothe aching joints and sciatica. A poultice, made from the roots and leaves boiled in water and applied as hot as possible to the hip, is an effective pain reliever, especially if the sufferer also drinks Goutweed tea.

Aegopodum podagraria photographed 10 June

Wild Pansy photographed 11 May

Wild Pansy or Heartsease

Viola tricolor, an annual or perennial, is common in Britain on hedgebanks and waste places. It grows to 30 cm. The flowers vary in colour and combinations of white, yellow and purple and blossom throughout the summer. They protect themselves from rain and dew by drooping their heads at night and in wet weather. Sow seeds out of doors in early spring. The plant was commonly associated with love, as local names **Love-in-Idleness** and **Kiss-me-Quick** suggest and it is the flowers that were used as a love-charm in Shakespeare's *Midsummer Night's Dream*. It is used to relieve rheumatism, dropsy and skin diseases. Gather the whole plant in summer and make a decoction in the following way. Add 50 grams of the dried plant to a litre of water, soak for an hour, then bring to the boil and infuse for ten minutes. Drink three or four glasses a day between meals. Apply compresses, soaked in the decoction.

Viola tricolor photographed 10 May

Marsh Mallow photographed 3 August

Marsh Mallow

Althaea officinalis, a native perennial, is found in salt marches, damp meadows and ditches by the coast in southern England. It grows to 1 metre and flowers from July to September. Sow the seeds in moist soil in the autumn and protect them from frost during the winter.

The plant contains a large amount of mucilage, used for its softening action. A tea made from the leaves and flowers or a decoction made by soaking the root in tepid water for several hours and then heating can be drunk three times a day to soothe chest complaints, relieve constipation and heal bladder infections. As a gargle it eases sore throats. The grated root mixed with honey and heated is used on poultices to reduce swelling. Roots were given to children to suck to relieve sore gums and the juice was used to flavour marshmallow sweets.

Althaea officinalis photographed 3 August

Lady's Mantle photographed 2 June

Lady's Mantle

Alchemilla vulgaris, a perennial native to northern Europe, is common on high-lying ground in the north of Britain. It grows to 30 cm and flowers from June to August. Sow the seeds during the spring. The robust, softly hairy Lady's Mantle commonly grown in gardens is *Alchemilla mollis*, native of the Carpathians.

Lady's Mantle was highly prized as a wound herb to stop bleeding. A decoction was made from the leaves and flowers, gathered in July, and used to bathe injuries. Culpepper advocated, 'the distilled water drunk for twenty days together, helps conception, and to retain the birth, if women do sometime sit in a bath made of the decoction of the herb'. This might explain why the plant is known as **Woman's Best Friend**. Today, herbalists use the plant to cure excessive menstruation and they apply juice extracted from the leaves to help clear acne. A sprig placed under the pillow is reputed to induce sleep.

Alchemilla vulgaris photographed 20 June

Comfrey photographed 27 May

Comfrey

Symphytum officinale, a perennial native of Europe and temperate Asia, thrives in damp meadows and shady places by rivers and streams throughout Britain. It grows to 80 cm. The cream, yellow, pink or purple flowers bloom from May to October. Cultivate by root division or seed during the autumn. A reputable medicinal herb, it is used as an astringent to arrest bleeding. A poultice made from crushed leaves cleans wounds, reduces swelling and bruising and unites fractured bones, hence its local name **Knitbone** and **Bruisewort**. A tea, made by immersing the roots and leaves in boiling water, is drunk to soothe chest complaints and ease coughs. The young leaves, finely chopped, can be scattered over salads, cooked like spinach or used in Comfrey fritters, made by dipping the whole leaves in batter and deep frying for two or three minutes. It is an ideal composting plant as it causes the rapid breakdown of other plant material. *Warning*: Repeated doses of Comfrey may be dangerous.

Symphytum officinale photographed 27 May

Valarian photographed 3 July

Valarian

Valariana officinalis, a native perennial, is found in marshy thickets, damp meadows and riversides throughout Britain. It grows to 1.2 metres and flowers from June to September. Sow seeds under glass in spring and transplant into damp, well-drained soil in a sunny position in summer or propagate by root division.

Valarian is a renowned herbal sedative. Only the root is used. When the plants are two years old gather the rhizomes in the autumn and dry in the dark. They have a fetid smell which cats find attractive and it sends them into a frenzy. A tea made from the dried root is taken to relieve tense headaches and to calm the nerves and if drunk an hour before going to bed will induce peaceful sleep. Although a soothing herb it should not be taken over long periods or in large doses because it produces pains in the head. Applied as a lotion it heals sores and skin rashes.

Valariana officinalis photographed 3 July

Deadly Nightshade photographed 20 August

Deadly Nightshade

Atropa bella-donna, a perennial, is widely distributed over Europe and south-west Asia, and is found on calcareous soil in the southeast of England. It grows to 1.25 metres and flowers from June to August, fruiting from August to November.

The shiny, juicy black berries look enticing to children but they are deadly poisonous, hence the plants local names: **Devil's Berries** or **Satan's Cherries**. Seventeenth century herbalist Gerard, after witnessing three deaths caused by eating the fruit urges, 'banish therefore these pernicious plants out of your gardens and all places near to your house where children do resort'. Deadly Nightshade is grown commercially, the leaves and roots being harvested in the second or third year, and sent to pharmaceutical companies to extract an alkaloid, atropine, a drug used to dilate the pupil of the eye.

Atropa-bella donna photographed 3 August

Eyebright photographed 3 August

Eyebright

Euphrasia officinalis, a small annual, is common on heaths and grassy places throughout Britain. It grows to 20 cm and flowers from June to September. The deeply cut, dark green leaves are usually lance-shaped and the white flowers are streaked with purple and yellow. It is a semi-parasitic relying on the roots of other plants for part of its nourishment, which can make it difficult to cultivate.

Greek fables claim that it was the linnet who first made use of Eyebright leaves to clear the sight of its young and they passed on the plant's virtues to mankind. This medicinal herb, as the name implies, is used as a remedy for eye infections. Make an infusion by adding 25 grams of the herb, either fresh or dried, to a pint of boiling water; when cool bathe the eyes three or four times a day. Eyebright tea is drunk as a tonic.

Euphrasia officinalis photographed 3 August

Self-heal photographed 3 August

Self-heal

Prunella vulgaris, a native perennial, is common in pastures, waste places and as a garden weed. It grows to 20 cm. The thick tiers of purple flowers blossom from June to September. Cultivate by planting rooted pieces of the runners, 5 cm deep, in spring or autumn.

Culpepper explained the name, 'Self-Heal whereby when you were hurt, you may heal yourself', and other local names; **All-Heal** and **Touch-and-Heal** suggest the herb was used to cure all wounds. Today's herbalists use it as an astringent. An infusion, made by adding 25 grams of the herb to a pint of boiling water, is used to cleanse cuts and reduce bruising. If sweetened with honey and taken in small doses (2 to 3 tablespoons), it relieves sore throats and mouth ulcers. The herb's juices mixed with rose oil are used to make a compress which can be applied to the forehead to soothe headaches.

Prunella vulgaris photographed 3 August

Vervain photographed 10 August

Vervain
Verbena officinalis, a native perennial, is common in the south of England
and Wales on wood edges, road verges and waste places. It grows to 50 cm
and flowers from June to September. Sow the seeds during spring in rich,
well-drained soil.

An important magic herb, it is employed by sorcerers and magicians to
foretell the future and cast or lift spells. A branch was hung above
doorways to ward off evil spirits. The plant was added to love-potions
because of its aphrodisiac qualities. Vervain necklaces were worn to soothe
headaches and bring good luck and even today some children wear sprigs
of the leaves to induce high spirits and good humour. Medicinally, Vervain
tea, made from the dried plant and pre-soaked in cold water for 15 minutes
then heated, is administered to relieve liver, kidney and bladder disorders.
As a gargle it eases sore throats and clears bad breath.

Verbena officinalis photographed 10 August

Foxglove photographed 14 June

Foxglove

Digitalis purpurea, a native biennial, has strong roots which sometimes produce flowers for several seasons. It thrives in woods, meadows, rocky places and roadsides. It grows to 1.5 metres and flowers from June to September. Cultivate by seed sown during April in light, well-drained soil and in partial shade.

Foxgloves are poisonous. It was considered the plant of fairies – the mottled markings on the blossoms were supposed to be elves' fingerprints, but since the discovery of the drug digitalin, the herb has become renowned for healing cardiac diseases. The flowers of the true medicinal plant must be dull pink or magenta. The leaves are harvested from two-year-old plants, while they are in bloom and sent to pharmaceutical companies. The drug slows down and strengthens the heart-beat, reduces blood pressure and makes the kidneys work more efficiently. Only take under medical supervision.

Digitalis purpurea photographed 14 June

Madagascar Periwinkle photographed 9 July

Madagascar Periwinkle

Catharanthus roseus, often called *Vinca rosea*, is a tropical slightly shrubby native of Madagascar, commonly grown for ornament in greenhouses and in gardens, in warm and especially in desert climates. It is almost continually in flower, with pale pink, purple or white petals and a darker eye.

Extracts from Madagascar periwinkle have recently been found to cure some types of leukaemia, in which there is a proliferation of white blood cells. A Canadian team of doctors, investigating its use as a herbal remedy against arthritis in the West Indies, found that laboratory mice died after being injected with an extract, and discovered that their white blood cells had been all but destroyed. This led to them to test the possible use of the Periwinkle against leukaemia.

Madagascar Periwinkle photographed 9 July

Greater Periwinkle photographed 30 April

Greater and Lesser Periwinkle

Vinca major and *Vinca minor*, evergreen perennials, were probably introduced but are well-established in woods, copses and hedgerows in the British Isles, rare in Ireland and the north. The creeping stems grow to 60 cm. Flowers which are deep purple-blue or white, as in a variety of Lesser Periwinkle, bloom from March to June. These common garden plants are cultivated to provide ground cover. Medicinally, Periwinkles are used as a tonic and an astringent to staunch haemorrhages. It was reputed to prevent miscarriages if a pregnant woman wore it fastened round her thigh. An infusion of the leaves makes an excellent gargle to relieve sore throats and inflamed tonsils. An ointment of the bruised leaves mixed with lard clears skin infections and is a good remedy for piles.

Greater and Lesser Periwinkle photographed 30 April

Gentian photographed 26 July

Gentian

Gentiana lutea is a perennial from alpine and sub-alpine meadows of central and southern Europe. It grows to 1.25 metres and flowers during the summer. Sow the seeds in cold frames then transplant seedlings to a rich, loamy soil in a sheltered position. Plants will take three years to grow to flowering size.

The yellowish-brown root, about 30 cm long and 3 cm in diameter is used medicinally. It is a powerful, bitter, vegetable tonic taken to revive the body after chronic illness, aid digestion and stimulate the appetite. The rhizomes are gathered in autumn, cut into slices and slowly dried. A tincture can be made by steeping 50 grams of the root, 25 grams of dried orange peel and 12 grams of bruised cardomon seeds in a litre of brandy. This is an excellent stomach tonic but must not be taken by people with high blood pressure or pregnant women. The root is a common ingredient in aperitifs and liqueurs.

Gentian photographed 26 July

Elecampane photographed 10 July

Elecampane
Inula helenium, a perennial from Europe and northern Asia can be found as
a garden escape in Britain. It grows to 1.5 metres and flowers from June to
August. Sow the seeds in spring in a moist, shady position or propagate by
root division. It is an attractive herbaceous plant.

A popular herb during the Middle Ages, its roots were candied and
eaten as sweets or an infusion was made and drunk as a general tonic. Only
the root is used. It is dug during the autumn from two or three-year-old
plants and dried. The aromatic scent and taste can be employed to flavour
desserts but as Culpepper suggests, it is most effective when the root is
made into a conserve or syrup, for settling an upset stomach, easing a stitch
in the side, relieving irritant coughs and shortness of breath. Steeped in
wine it is a stimulant and powerful vermifuge and as a gargle it is supposed
to help fasten loose teeth.

Inula helenium photographed 10 July

Blessed Thistle photographed 5 August

Blessed Thistle

Cnicus benedictus is an annual from southern Europe where it grows wild on stony and uncultivated places. It grows to 60 cm and flowers from June to August. Sow the seeds in spring in any soil and when the seedlings appear, thin-out, allowing 60 cm between each plant.

The name 'Blessed Thistle' was given to the herb for its medicinal virtues to 'heal-all'; it is even reputed to have cured the plague. The Romans used the whole plant: they boiled the roots, added the young leaves to salads and prepared and served the flower heads like globe artichokes. Herbalists now use the fresh plant as a tonic and diaphoretic or dried and powdered as a vermifuge. A warm infusion of the flowers and leaves is given to nursing mothers to induce a proper supply of milk but only use in small doses as it can be a stomach irritant.

Cnicus benedictus photographed 5 August

Feverfew photographed 17 June

Feverfew

Chrysanthemum parthenium, a perennial from southeast Europe and Asia Minor, is abundant throughout Britain on waste places, hedgerows and roadsides. It grows to 5 cm and flowers from July to August. Sow the seeds under glass in March then plant out in early June in well-drained soil or propagate by root division.

Feverfew, as the name implies, was used as a popular remedy for dispelling fevers and as a general tonic. An infusion, made by steeping the flowers in boiling water and allowed to cool, is drunk to cure headaches and earache. A tincture made from the herb acts as an insect repellent or applied to bites and stings instantly relieves pain and reduces swelling. At one time, pots of Feverfew placed on their sides were dotted around the garden to provide shelter for toads who in return ate all the slugs.

Chrysanthemum parthenium photographed 17 June

Arnica seedheads photographed 5 August

Arnica

Arnica montana, a perennial, native in woods and mountain meadows of central Europe, is occasionally found in Britain as a garden escape. It grows to 50 cm and flowers from July to August. Sow the seeds under glass in March and plant out in May or propagate by root division in the spring.

The flowers gathered during the summer and the roots collected in autumn can be infused in water or steeped in alcohol and applied externally. The tincture is used to ease sprains, reduce bruising, heal wounds and as a foot bath to soothe aching feet. However, repeated application of the mixture may cause severe skin inflammation. This plant should not be taken internally because some people are allergic to it and fatal cases of poisoning have resulted. At one time the leaves were gathered, dried and smoked as a substitute for tobacco, hence its popular name, Mountain Tobacco.

Arnica photographed 10 July

Lily-of-the-Valley photographed 6 May

Lily-of-the-Valley

Convallaria majalis, a native rhizome of Europe, is a rare wild plant in Britain but can occasionally be found in dry woods, especially ash woods. It grows to 30 cm and flowers from May to June, producing poisonous berries from August to September. Cultivate by root division in September and it will then thrive in a well-drained, rich, sandy loam.

A potentially poisonous plant, it contains a glucoside, Convallamarin, which is a remedy for cardiac complaints. It is similar to the drug Digitalin but it is less powerful. An infusion, made with 2 grams of dried flowers to 100 grams of boiling water and allowed to brew for five minutes, then sweetened with honey, acts as a sedative and tonic by calming the nerves and regulating and strengthening the heart beat. It is also a diuretic. The dried flowers, powdered and taken like snuff, are supposed to relieve headaches and earaches and heal eye infections.

Convallaria majalis photographed 6 May

Male Fern photographed 10 May

Male Fern

Dryopteris filix-mas, a native rhizome, is one of the commonest British ferns, thriving in damp woods, shady places, moist banks and hedgerows. The fronds can grow up to 90 cm. Spores ripen during July and August. An oil extracted from the rhizome is a powerful vermifuge. The remedy for expelling tapeworms became famous when Louis XVI paid Madame Nouffer 1,800 francs to publish her secret recipe – an infusion made by adding 12 grams of the powdered root to 190 grams of lime blossom water. Today the oil extract is taken last thing at night after several hours' fasting, followed by a caster oil purgative taken first thing in the morning. One dose is usually sufficient to remove all traces of worms. In some country areas the leaves are placed in mattresses and pillows because they are reputed to have anti-rheumatic virtues. They are also said to cure children of rickets and stop them wetting the bed.

Dryopteris felix-mas photographed 10 July

INDEX

Achillea millefolium 96
Adderwort 80
Aegopodium podagraria 118
Alchemilla, mollis 124
    vulgaris 124
Alecost 68
All-heal 134
Allium, sativum 88
    schoenoprasum 90
Althaea officinalis 122
American Mandrake 110
Anethum graveolens 46
Angelica 74
Angelica archangelica 74
Anise 42
Anthemis nobilis 92
Anthriscus cerefolium 48
Apium, graveolens 40
    var. dulce 40
    nodiflorum 40
    var. rapaceum 40
Apple Mint 12
Armoracia rusticana 54
Arnica 152
Arnica montana 152
Artemisa absinthium 98
Artemisia dracunculus 52
Atropa bella-donna 130
Basil, Bush 24
    Sweet 26
    Purple 26
Bay 60
Bee Balm 102
Bergamot 102
Bibleleaf 68
Bistort 80
Blessed Thistle 148
Borage 56
Borago officinalis 56
Bowles Mint 12
Bronze Fennel 34
Bruisewort 126
Burnet, Greater 86
    Salad 86
Bush Basil 24
Calendula officinalis 66
Capsella bursa-pastoris 72
Caraway 42
Carum carvi 42
Catharanthus roseus 140
Celandine, Greater 112
    Lesser 112
Celeriac 40
Celery 40
Chamomilla recutita 92
Chamomile, Double-centred 92
    Lawn 92
Chelidonium majus 112
Chervil 48
Chicory 64
Chives 90

Chrysanthemum balsamita 68
    parthenium 150
Cichovium intybus 64
Clary 20
Cnicus benedictus 148
Coltsfoot 94
Comfrey 126
Common Sorrel 78
Common Thyme 6
Convallaria majalis 154
Coriander 38
Coriandrum sativum 38
Corsican Mint 16
Corn Mint 10
Costmary 68
Crocus sativus 58
Curly Leafed Parsley 32
Curly Mint 14
Dandelion 70
Deadly Nightshade 130
Devil's Berries 130
Digitalis purpurea 138
Dill 46
Dog Elder 118
Double-centred Chamomile 92
Dryopteris filix-mas 156
Dwarf Elder 118
Easter Ledge 80
Eau de Cologne Mint 14
Elder 104
Elder, Dog 118
    Dwarf 118
    Ground 118
Elecampane 146
Endive 64
Euphrasia officinalis 132
Eyebright 132
Fennel, Bronze 34
    Florence 34
Fenugreek 62
Feverfew 150
Field Mint 10
Foeniculum, vulgare 34
Fool's Watercress 40
Foxglove 138
French Parsley 32
French Sorrel 78
French Tarragon 52
Garden Thyme 6
Garlic 88
Gentian 144
Gentiana lutea 144
Ginger 62
Golden Purslane 84
    Thyme 6
Goutweed 118
Greater Burnet 86
Greater Celandine 112
    Periwinkle 142
Green Purslane 84
Ground Elder 118
Heartsease 120
Hemlock Water Dropwort 40
Horse Mint 10

Horseradish 54
Hyssop 28
Hyssopus officinalis 28
Inula helenium 146
Juniper 108
Juniperus communis 108
Kiss-me-quick 120
Knitbone 126
Lady's Mantle 124
Large Wild Thyme 4
Laurus nobilis 60
Lawn Chamomile 92
Lemon Balm 100
    Thyme 8
Lesser Celandine 112
    Periwinkle 142
Levisticum officinale 36
Lily-of-the-valley 154
Lime 106
Linden 106
Long Leafed Mint 14
Lovage 36
Love-in-idleness 120
Mace 68
Madagascar Periwinkle 140
Male Fern 156
Marigold 66
Marsh Mallow 122
May Apple 110
Melissa officinales 100
Mentha, Arvensis 10
    aquatica 10
    citrata 14
    crispa 14
    longifolia 10
    piperita 14
    pulegium 16
    requienii 16
    rotundifolia 12
    rotundifolia variegata 12
    spicata 14
Milfoil 96
Mint, Apple 12
    Bowles 12
    Corn 10
    Corsican 16
    Curly 14
    Eau de Cologne 14
    Field 10
    Horse 10
    Long Leafed 14
    Pennyroyal 16
    Peppermint 14
    Pineapple 12
    Round leafed 12
    Spearmint 14
    Water 10
    Wild 10
Monarda didyma 102
Mother's heart 72
Mother Thyme 4
Myrrhis odorata 44
Nasturtium 82
Ocimum, basilicum 26

minimum 24
Oenanthe crocata 40
Opium Poppy 114
Oregano 22
Origanum vulgare 22
Oswego Tea 102
Papaver somniferum 114
Parsley, Curly Leafed 32
   French 32
   Plain Leaved 32
Pennyroyal 16
Peppermint 14
Periwinkle, Greater 142
   Lesser 142
   Madagascar 140
Petroselinum crispum 32
Pilewort 112
Pimpinella anisum 42
Pineapple Mint 12
Plain-leaved Parsley 32
Podophyllum, emodi 110
   peltatum 110
Polygonum bistorta 80
Portulaca oleracea 84
Prunella vulgaris 134
Purple Basil 26
Purslane, Golden 84
   Green 84
Rosemary 30
Rosmarinus officinalis 30
Round-leafed mint 12
Rue 116
Rumex acetosa 78
Russian tarragon 52
Ruta graveolens 116
Saffron 58
Sage 18
Salad Burnet 86
Salvia, officinalis 18
   sclarea 20
Sambucus nigra 104
Sanguisorba, minor 86
   officinalis 86
Satan's cherries 130
Self-heal 134
Shepherd's Purse 72
Sium sisarum 76
Skirret 76
Snakeweed 80
Sorrel, Common 78
   French 78
Spearmint 14
Sweet Basil 26
Sweet Cecily 44
Symphytum offinale 126
Tanacetum vulgare 50
Tansy 50
Taraxacum officinale 70
Tarragon, French 52
   Russian 52
Thyme, Common 6
   Garden 6
   Golden 6
   Large Wild 4

Lemon 8
Mother 4
Wild 4
Thymus, azoricus 6
   citriodorus 8
   drucei 4
   pulegioides 4
   serpyllum 4
   vulgaris 6
Tilia europaea 106
Touch and heal 134
Trigonella foenum-graecum 62
Tropaeolum majus 82
Tussilago farfara 94
Valarian 128
Valariana officinalis 128
Verbena officinalis 136
Vervain 136
Vinca, major 142
   minor 142
   rosea 140
Viola tricolor 120
Water Mint 10
Wild, Bergamot 102
   Marjoram 22
   Mint 10
   Pansy 120
   Succory 64
   Thyme 4
Witloaf 64
Woman's Best Friend 124
Wormwood 98
Yarrow 96
Zingiber officinale 62

Roger Phillips has pioneered the photography of natural history which ensures reliable identification. By placing each specimen against a plain background he is able to show details that would otherwise have been lost if it had been photographed solely *in situ*. Such is the success of his technique that his books, which include the definitive guide to *Mushrooms*, *Wild Food* and *Freshwater Fish*, have sold over a million copies worldwide. He is also the winner of numerous awards, including three for best produced and best designed books and the André Simon prize for 1983 for *Wild Food*.

Jacqui Hurst studied photography at Gloucestershire College of Art & Design, worked as an assistant to Roger Phillips for 4 years, and is now a freelance journalist and photographer, specializing in country matters.

Martyn Rix took a degree in botany in Trinity College, Dublin and then went on to Cambridge. After a further period of study in Zurich he became resident botanist at the Royal Horticultural Society's gardens at Wisley for several years. He is now a freelance writer.

Acknowledgements
We should like to thank the Chelsea Physic Garden, its curator Duncan Donald and head gardener, James Compton, for their help and for many of the herbs shown here; also Hollington Nurseries, near Newbury, and the RHS Garden, Wisley, for other specimens.

Other titles in this series:

Coastal Wild Flowers

Seashells and Seaweeds

Wild Flowers of Roadsides and Waste Places

garden and field
Weeds

native and common
Trees

common and important
Mushrooms

woodland
Wild Flowers

First published in Great Britain 1987
by Elm Tree Books/Hamish Hamilton Ltd
27 Wrights Lane London W8 5TZ

Copyright © 1987 by Roger Phillips

Cover design by Pat Doyle

ISBN 0241-12060-8
ISBN 0241-12029-2 Pbk

Typeset by Rowland Phototypesetting Ltd
Bury St Edmunds, Suffolk
Printed in Great Britain by Cambus Litho